STARTING YOUR ONLINE BUSINESS

A Detailed Active Course Guide For You With Checklists and Tasks

Platinum Publishing

WELCOME

The proactive guide that will help you set up your online business

In this dynamic digital age, where technology's magic touches every aspect of your life, it's no surprise that the internet has become a fertile ground for the sprouting of various business endeavors. Small businesses can flourish online if done right.

The world of online business is teeming with opportunities. Whether you envision an e-commerce store bustling with customers, a blog transforming into a revenue-generating platform, or a virtual assistant business that provides remote services, the digital landscape invites you with open arms, promising endless possibilities.

With this guide, we'll dive deep into the nitty-gritty of launching your digital venture. Our chapters break down some of the most complex business concepts into digestible, actionable steps. I'm here to turn that dream of yours into something real and achievable.

I also firmly believe in the power of staying organized. To that end, my course includes checklists for each step of your business setup, and I add some fun into the mix for well-deserved breaks.

So, prepare for an exciting adventure into the online business world. Together, we'll navigate the path to success, ensuring you have a clear roadmap and an enjoyable journey. And remember, even if this venture isn't wildly successful, it can take you into the next venture that could be.

Here's to the start of something great!

TABLE OF CONTENTS

TABLE OF CONTENTS

CHAPTER 1
THE ENTREPRENEUR MINDSET

To understand the entrepreneurial mindset, you must first understand the employee mindset and see the contrast between the two mindsets.

About the Employee Mindset

The Employee Mindset is a conditioning. From the time we are five or six years old and enter the school system, we are told when to be there, what to do, how to do it, when we can go to lunch, and when we can go home.

Over and over and over and over again, we go through this cycle. Every day... kindergarten...first grade...second grade...every day, through graduation.

We are taught that others manage our time and our activities. When we enter the workforce, we are told when to be there, what to do, when to do it, when we can go to lunch (if we can go...), and when we can go home. T

This might be at 14, 16, or 18 years old; perhaps some of you have gone on to college and maybe do not start your first job until you are 22 years old.

It all works the same, and it is all the same mindset. In a job, when we run out of work, it's a subconscious passive thought process. We sit back and wait for further instructions. We might surf the internet, make a few phone calls, answer a few emails, take a break, and wait for our boss to tell us the next thing we need to do.

If you are self-employed or starting your own business, can you afford to sit back and wait for further instruction? You would go out of business before even getting started.

If you don't know what to do next, what do you do? Who or where would you get further instruction from?

About the Entrepreneur Mindset

Starting and running a successful business takes the Entrepreneur Mindset, which is a much more proactive mindset.

If you don't know what to do, then you figure it out. You get further instruction from yourself. You make phone calls, and you get a coach or mentor; you call the local chamber of commerce, you go to networking events, ask questions, surf the internet, search YouTube, call the state office building, and contact the SBA (Small Business Administration) until you find your answer.

You don't wait for your business associates, your upline, or anyone else to give you the answers. You find the answers on your own. The essence of the Entrepreneurial Mindset is ownership of your circumstances, control of your time, and understanding that you always have choices in any given situation.

You own what you do, you own your decisions, you own your failures, and most importantly,
You own your successes.

What Are the Differences Between the Mindsets?

Let's say you come up with a good idea for your job, and you share the idea with your boss, and that idea saves the company a lot of money. The company experiences a 10% profit increase in the next quarter. Yay, company!

But do you see a dime of the 10% profit increase in your next paycheck? You do not own that success; the company you work for owns that success. You feel employment security.

Let's look at the flip side of this coin. Let's say you are working at a job and find out at 4:45 p.m. that you are losing your job. There have been layoffs, and the company is filing bankruptcy.

You're not coming back to work the next day. You spend the remaining 15 minutes cleaning out your desk, putting your stuff in a box, never to see that desk again, never to return to that job again. I've been there; many of you may have been there, too.

It's scary, it's sad...you are worried about where your next car payment is coming from or where next week's groceries are coming from. You know you will be revamping your resume', beating the streets begging for interviews, 12 hours a day, hoping you will get another job. You may get another job in a few days... a few weeks...or a few months... or longer.

However... You can walk away from that job knowing you do not own that failure.

This is the essence of the Employee Mindset. The jobs that I was let go from, I knew I did not own that failure and that I could go out there and get another job, and I did, very quickly, in fact. Each time I was let go, I would first be somewhat sad and scared.

Then, I would look at the near future as an opportunity to make some decisions about my part-time business and my full-time work. Each and every time, I would find a better job or position, and it eventually led me to begin working from home with the flexibility that I so truly wanted in the long run.

In fact, I remember working as a paralegal at a large law firm in downtown Salt Lake City. I was only making hundreds each month off of two websites I had built within the prior two years. I wanted to help teach people what I had learned in web building and getting traffic. I was not happy working in a law firm anymore.

I scanned the newspaper classifieds looking for a job that I could transition into that would allow me to teach others what I knew about internet marketing. I found one. It said, "Internet Marketing Coach Needed." I thought to myself...WOW, that is exactly what I am looking to do!

I sent in my resume/bio and got an interview that I drove 2 ½ hours to get to. The interview lasted two hours, and by the time I got home, I had an offer on my answering machine to start taking on clients. Yes! I accepted and put in my two weeks' notice at that legal job.

That was the first time I was actually able to begin working from home. It wasn't just a job, I was running my own business and making a full time income working only 20 hours a week. However, I was still stuck in the Employee Mindset. I will explain...

In the Entrepreneurial Mindset, you own every success and every failure, and you are in control of how you respond to all things in your environment.

Some of you may not like to hear that. You are not stuck where you are, you do not have to stay in that job, or any situation, for that matter, if you do not want to. You own your circumstances and your choices.

You are NOT a victim.

Therefore, you have the power to control your circumstances and the power to control your direction. The company I was working with to get internet marketing clients and work from home lasted about 18 months, and they went out of business.

We had a scheduled coaching meeting to go into the office on the last Friday of every month. I drove 2 ½ hours to get to that meeting to find the doors locked and a "For Rent" sign out in front of the building.

No wonder I had run out of clients! They did not tell me they were going out of business. Every time I called to find out about the sales slump, I was told that the sales staff were getting more training and that it was just a slow time of year. In all actuality, they were going out of business, and I was out of clients, and I didn't know what to do. So, I did nothing. I was stuck in the Employee Mindset.

I then began to apply for legal jobs, got one in downtown Salt Lake City again, and had to return to the office.

A few months into my new job, I received a call from the head coach of that prior company. He had started his own coaching company and wanted me to coach the clients that were coming on board. I began to bring on clients part-time to make ends meet and continue working my day job.

This individual also began to coach me every week and helped me understand more about the Entrepreneur Mindset. At one point between these weekly calls, I had a big A-HA moment.

It felt like my internal universe imploded and then exploded. I had the sensation of a trembling earthquake that took over my entire being, body, soul, and emotions. I had to hang on to the edges of my desk for several moments while this A-HA moment happened. It was a huge shift.

I had transitioned from the Employee Mindset to the Entrepreneurial Mindset.

During those moments, I realized that I am responsible for everything that has happened, is happening, and will happen to me and my life. Not only am I responsible, but I also own it. I own every success and every failure. Also, during those moments, my memories of all the events where I saw myself as a victim were completely restructured.

Memories of love gone wrong, boyfriends and fiancée having cheated on me, my Mother, my Father, my sister, my best friend who betrayed me. All of it was forgiven, and so much love poured out of me. I took responsibility and ownership of my part in all of those events, and I realized that every one of them did the best they could under their current circumstances...and so had I.

Many people whom I have coached through making this same shift do not feel this "earthquake" but more of a gradual and subtle change. A few have felt the earthquake. I am not sure how it may happen to you.

You may be one of those people who have already made the shift; however, there are many levels that you can achieve within the Entrepreneurial Mindset, and the process is still the same.

How To Take Back Your Control

In order to make this shift, there are two tools that most successful entrepreneurs have learned to use and master. Do what successful entrepreneurs do...incorporate these two tools into your arsenal, and you will become successful, too.

So, what are these two tools? A written time management system and a journal. They seem simple and basic, but they are the two critical tools that will build the bridge between the Employee Mindset and the Entrepreneurial Mindset.

Time Management – Get Different Results

This means you must use your time differently. We all work with the same 24 hours; some of us just get more done than others. The difference is the effective use of time management. The most effective way to change the use of your time is to plan it and manage it...in writing. Some may refer to this as "activity" management. Either way, it's still the same.

Take Control – Plan Your Time

You will now need to plan into your week the actual number of hours you have committed and dedicated to your business. For some of you, this may be 8 hours a week; for others, it may be 30 or more.

If you do not take control of your time, I guarantee you that your week will blow by you like a whirlwind. Suddenly, before you know it, weeks or months will have gone by, and you will look back and see that you haven't accomplished a whole lot because "life happens."

Life also happens to successful entrepreneurs; they still get their stuff done. Then, all your excuses, which are often called "reasons," come up so you can feel better about not getting to your business and creating the success you want.

Whenever I ask a coaching client how things went for them that week, I get the answer, "Busy!" That is code for, "I didn't get much done." With that in mind, here are a couple of helps.

Remember, you are in business or going into business, so you can be "in control." You want control of your financial future, time, and flexibility. You want to be your own boss – work when you want, do what you want when you want, all of that, right?

Well, the first tool to use to get in control and stay in control is planning your time. If you do not plan your time, you automatically default to "out of control."

Time Management & Planning

For time management and planning, get a planner that has a day-at-a-glance, not a week, not a month, but a day-at-a-glance. This means a sheet per day with hourly segments. This will give you enough room to schedule your days in hour-to-hour increments. This is the layout that works for 95% of entrepreneurs. For the other 5%, an electronic time management tool works, such as your phone calendar.

At the beginning of each week, commit to a number of hours you will work your business, 10, 15, 20, etc. Write your weekly commitment down in your planner.

Schedule the days of your week and the specific hours of each day that you will be working on your business. For instance, Tuesday from 6:00 a.m. to 8:00 a.m., Wednesday from 5:00 p.m. to 10:00 p.m., etc.

Make sure you write out your schedule in your calendar or planner. Do not rely on your memory. Doing your business when you have time, if you have time, is a hobby. What do hobbies pay?

Entrepreneurs do not rely on their memory; they write it all down and track it. It is important you keep these appointments with yourself, like you would any other person you respect and take seriously (doctor, Lawyer, CPA).

If you find yourself breaking your appointments with yourself, ask yourself, "What am I telling myself about me and this business?" We all make time for those things that are truly important to us.

Next, make a "To Do" list for the week. Prioritize that list. Assign an amount of time to complete each item, then double or triple that amount. This will give you extra time, or buffer time, so you do not go into panic and crisis mode if things do not move as smoothly as you would like.

Implement your plan day by day. If you see you are not completing your plan for the time period you set up each week, schedule yourself more time to get it done.

Remember, this is your business. If you do not do it, who will?

The Second Step In Taking Control - Using a Journal

About Your Journal

The journal is a tool to assist you in learning how to think independently, instigate your own activities, and create success in your life. It's about not relying on external guidance and/or influence for you to make decisions that serve you, your business, and your greater good.

For you to do that, you must be able to think clearly and specifically. This leads to clarity of motivation, thought, problem-solving, decision-making, goal setting, planning and time management, follow through, and the successful achievement of your goals.

Goals are most often not achieved without this clarity. Your journal is the tool of all tools, the record, and portfolio of your implementation and successes. What are the uses of a journal, or what are the tools to be used in it?

Diary writing – recording the events of the day.
Free associative writing – doing a brain dump, writing whatever comes to mind without editing – let it flow; you may be surprised by what you learn and discover.
Verbally vomiting – when you have had a bad day, bad experience, just frustrated and feeling confused or overwhelmed – put it here and let it go.
Imagining and daydreaming – let your mind dream and paint the pictures of your success and accomplishments.
Brainstorming or idea generation – coming up with ideas, alternatives, options, and possibilities.
Researching – collecting information and data from books, the Internet, what others say, etc.
Problem-solving – put your problem-solving processes and procedures in here to work it out and give yourself objectivity.
Decision making – clarify your objective/goal, weigh the possibilities and outcomes, and find the best decision.
Goal setting – what do you want, and when do you want it?
Planning and time management – what is the plan to get there, how to do it, what to do, when to do it, and by whom (time management then gets transferred to a separate planner).
Tracking – measuring progress and improvements.
Refinement – how to work smarter; how to get better outcomes.
Setbacks – determining what did not work, corrections, new planning, and implementation.
Success – What happened, what worked? How did you do it? Celebrate it.
Wisdom and insight – what have you learned from what you have read, researched, planned, implemented, achieved, etc.
Gratitude – Some of you who are already familiar with the Law of Attraction know about a gratitude journal. This doesn't have to be a separate journal. You can incorporate your gratitude writing right into your journal.

A very honest conversation with you is what a journal is all about. You then apply creative problem-solving, imagination, desire, and passion to your goals. Then, you add the will to figure out how to get on with your goals, doing it and achieving it.

There are two areas of management you must consistently manage: Yourself and your time. If you do not manage yourself or your time, you cannot manage much of anything, let alone your goals. It is that simple.

So, in your journal, you have a conversation with yourself about you.

- How am I doing?
- What am I doing?
- Where am I going?
- What am I getting done?
- How well am I doing it?
- What am I achieving?
- When will I have it done?
- What can I improve?
- Where am I stuck?
- What are my long-term goals?
- What are my quarterly, monthly, weekly, and daily goals?
- Do I have plans of action in place to implement?
- Am I getting it done?
- How do I feel about all of it?
- What kind of difference am I making for myself and others?
- What am I grateful for?
- What did I do well today?

Setting up Your Journal

Since your journal is something you work in, record in, plan in, etc., and go back and review weekly, you should have something that is going to last over time.

In my opinion, a three-ring binder is perfect for this. When you fill it up with paper and writing, get another binder.

A tablet of paper is not likely to work well with this; neither is a spiral-bound notebook. A book-bound journal might work, but it's not my favorite. The idea is something that will last, is easy to write in, and carry with you when necessary.

If you like to write on your computer, then that may work, too. If you like to carry your journal around with you as well, then you will have to be a bit more innovative.

Either transcribe your written notes into your computer or print out your typed-in words to put into your three-ring binder. I would pick one or the other to make this easier.

The point is, that you want it all in one place for work and reference; that is what will create your best focus and results.

How Often You Should Write

Two times a day, minimum, once in the morning, once at night. More often, if you really need to.

Just like the dentist tells you to brush your teeth at least twice a day, incorporate your journal writing the same way. It is as critical to your "business health" as brushing your teeth is to your dental health.

What would happen if you didn't brush your teeth for a few weeks? Ewwwwww, decay, fuzzy teeth, really bad breath, right?

The same thing with your journal. Your business will not make the kind of progress it could make unless you consistently have the clarity the daily journal writing will bring you.

So, the point is, do not let your journal get bad breath. Write in it daily, and only then will you truly realize the power you can harness with this simple tool.

CHAPTER 1 HOMEWORK

A huge part of being an entrepreneur is about having the right attitude—the kind that keeps you going, allows you to think of your mistakes as lessons learned, and overcome obstacles.

Learn from the best of them

Being resilient, not being scared to take risks, and having a creative streak are super important in the entrepreneurial world. Set aside some time to read about or listen to podcasts from successful entrepreneurs—trust me, their stories are far from boring.

- [ ] Find a successful entrepreneur that resonates this you. This can be someone you already know of or a new person that you find interesting.
- [ ] Search for books or podcasts from these people or that feature these people and their stories.
- [ ] Set aside a good amount of to listen to/read their stories. Take note of anything that piques your interest.

Create your 'growth mindset'

Next up, let's work on creating what we call a 'growth mindset'. This is all about believing that you're not just stuck with the abilities you have now. No matter what you tell yourself, with some good old dedication and hard work, you can become better at most things!

- [ ] Set Fun Learning Goals: Don't worry about being perfect at something. Instead, focus on learning and experiencing new things. Set up your time management and journal.
- [ ] Grab a good book or find a podcast to help you build your growth mindset.
- [ ] Speak nicely to yourself. You're doing great. Whenever you start to doubt, remind yourself of that.

Learn from mistakes

Get yourself ready for some bumps in the road. Things might not always go as planned, and that's okay! Each failure is just a way to learn something new. Remember, every time you fall and get back up, you're one step closer to your goal.

- [ ] Write down in your journal how you overcame issues and what you will do differently next time.

Create your schedule

You will need to build some discipline and be able to manage your time. Being an entrepreneur means you're your own boss and you will have to make your own schedules and stick to them, handle all kinds of tasks, and keep yourself motivated without anyone else telling you what to do or giving you a helping hand.

- [ ] Find a calendar/task system that will work for you to plan your working day
- [ ] Time your repeating tasks so you have a good idea of how long tasks will take you.
- [ ] Print out a favorite quote or anything that will give you a boost when you start to lose focus.

Task Checklist

- [ ] I understood the entrepreneur mindset and took notes for my own journey.
- [ ] I focused on my growth mindset.
- [ ] I am braced and ready for failures (and excited about learning from them).
- [ ] I have worked on my discipline, journal and time management.

CHAPTER 2 IDENTIFYING YOUR NICHE

The first step to creating an online business is to choose what kind of online business you want to create. This starts by choosing a niche – what is the subject matter you will be dealing with?

In this section, you will learn how to do this, and you will see how this initial decision goes on to influence every other step.

What is a Niche, and Why Does it Matter?

Every site should have a niche that describes the kind of thing that you will be writing about and the people you will be writing it for. Your site might be a 'general' site or a personal blog that doesn't stick to any particular topic, but even then, there will be at least a 'theme' or a feel tying it together. You might write about books, coffee, and the city, but that's still a niche in its way, and it's one that will attract a very specific type of person.

Knowing and understanding your niche is incredibly important if you hope to be able to make your site successful. Unfortunately, too many webmasters do not really fully understand their niche, and their sites tend to suffer as a result.

Essentially, you should know what your niche is. For most site owners or bloggers, this will be an incredibly easy question to answer: the site will probably be about 'football' or 'technology', and that's fairly easy to define.

If your site is more general, though, then make a list of all the topics that you write about regularly and then think about a) what ties them together and b) what kind of person will read them. You've probably created a new niche for yourself, but as long as your future content meets those same criteria, then you will be on the money.

The niche you pick should primarily be determined by your own interests. If you're going to be living and breathing your blog for the next ten years, then this NEEDS to be something you're keen to learn and write about.

What's more, you won't be able to deliver really unique and valuable content if you don't know anything about the topic! And hiring professional writers won't guarantee that you'll find someone who has a real passion and interest in the topic.

While that's true, you also need to consider the viability of the niche choice. How competitive is it? Do you stand a chance against the biggest sites? How profitable and monetizable is it? The subject you choose should be something that people are willing to spend money on and that has lots of opportunities for informational products.

Get More Specific When Choosing Your Niche

But in order to really succeed – and to gain an edge over the competition - you need to go a little deeper. Sure, your site might be a technology website, but what kind of technology do you write about? Who are you writing for? And what is the purpose of your site?

For instance, you might write about all kinds of technology but find that you seem to stick more to technology that's just around the corner. Perhaps you write lots of big previews for technology that's coming. And perhaps you write in a very technical way that is clearly aimed at people who know their stuff. This is a very different niche from a site that reviews basic commercial technology in a style that can appeal to the average customer. Again, then, you will have created your own niche that should be completely unique.

You might make a football site, sure, but is it a dry site that deals with a detailed overview of football for real fanatics? Or is it a more gossip-filled site that's aimed at the typical 'guy'?

Again, these are slightly different niches, and it's important to recognize the difference. If you can be consistent with your precise niche, then you will find that your site offers something that not every other site does. You will have a specific audience and people who particularly like the way you approach the topic. Stick to your guns, and you can make your site highly successful as a result.

The Power of Creating Your Own Niche

That said, though, there are a few niches left that have a good number of people interested but that nevertheless don't have too much overcrowding in the marketplace.

This is particularly difficult when you consider how important it also is that you actually be interested in the niche that you're going to be dealing with so regularly from now on and that you actually know a thing or two about it, too.

So, how do you stand out without limiting your appeal or writing about something dull? Well, one solution is to come up with your own niche and create a website that will be unlike any other. Here, we will look at how you can potentially accomplish that.

Sites That Don't Fit Nicely into Boxes

When you browse the web for inspiration on niches for your website, you will often find lists of categories such as 'fitness,' 'making money,' 'football,' 'film,' and others like these. Not every site, though, has to fit neatly into a category like this - it is possible to come up with a completely unique angle and create a niche that wasn't there before.

Take http://www.lifehacker.com, for instance, and http://www.lifehack.org. These sites exist in the same niche but go back a decade, and that niche wouldn't have existed. These sites tie together many themes using a 'way of life' or 'attitude' to gel it all together. In this case, that attitude is the 'hacker' attitude - where DIY applies to everything from self-improvement to making money, but you could just as easily build a site around any other central idea like this.

Bringing Various Concepts Together

If you can't find a new theme to link the items on your site, though, then another option is to simply combine multiple existing niches that you think will go well together.

This way, you have your built-in audience - because you'll get visitors from both of those existing niches - but at the same time, you will have your own unique USP and be able to offer something that's different from everything else.

Examples might include 'bodybuilding and self-improvement,' 'making money online and city living,' 'travel and art', or 'cafes, coffee, and books.'

Alternatively, just taking a broader approach with your stories can help to give your site more meat and put your niche more in context with other topics. This strategy is also effective because it creates a number of simple marketing options that you can use to reach a new audience. For instance, if you have a website based around bodybuilding and self-improvement, then you will be able to promote your site on self-improvement forums without being directly in competition with those sites.

Going More Niche

In contrast to broadening your niche, another option is to get even more specific by finding a category within a category. Again, this will allow you to market on sites that would otherwise see you as competition and will help make SEO easier by focusing your aim.

An example might be to target a particular kind of film, such as '80s action films', a particular era of music, or perhaps a particular kind of exercise, such as bodyweight training alone.

Trailblazing

Finally, if you have the resources, then you can even consider creating a niche before you create your website. For example, if you run a software company and you release a new piece of software or a new computer game, then you will likely find that this generates interest and fans.

By creating a website focusing on the software you have released, you can then provide an official website for that interest and create an almost symbiotic relationship between your software and your website where the success of one helps the success of the other. This works for every kind of product and service that will catch the public's attention. Though not every webmaster will have a product to promote, it's important that businesses and entrepreneurs don't miss this opportunity when it does present itself.

CHAPTER 2 HOMEWORK

Nailing down your niche is a little like a treasure hunt. It's all about unearthing that well-defined, targetable corner of the market where you can plant the seeds of your business. The more intimately you know your niche, the more effectively you can shape your product or service to fit their unique needs. You'll also be able to chat with them in their language, making your marketing efforts that much more successful.

Write down your passions, hobbies, and talents. Think about what really fires you up, and the areas where your knowledge or skills give you an edge.

Investigate the market to spot potential niches. Keep an eye out for those market gaps—places where there's a real craving for something, but it's just not being satisfied.

Now, it's time for some competition analysis. What's working for them? Where are they dropping the ball? Importantly, what unique improvement can you bring to the table?

The final step is all about honing in on a niche where you can deliver something genuinely different. Using your research, write down a summary of what you would like to offer or what problems you can solve and offer as a service or a product.

Task Checklist

- [ ] I have pinpointed my niche.
- [ ] I have explored and understood my competition.
- [ ] I have created a distinct value offering that sets me apart from the rest.

CHAPTER 3
DEVELOPING YOUR BUSINESS IDEA

This is where it gets exciting!

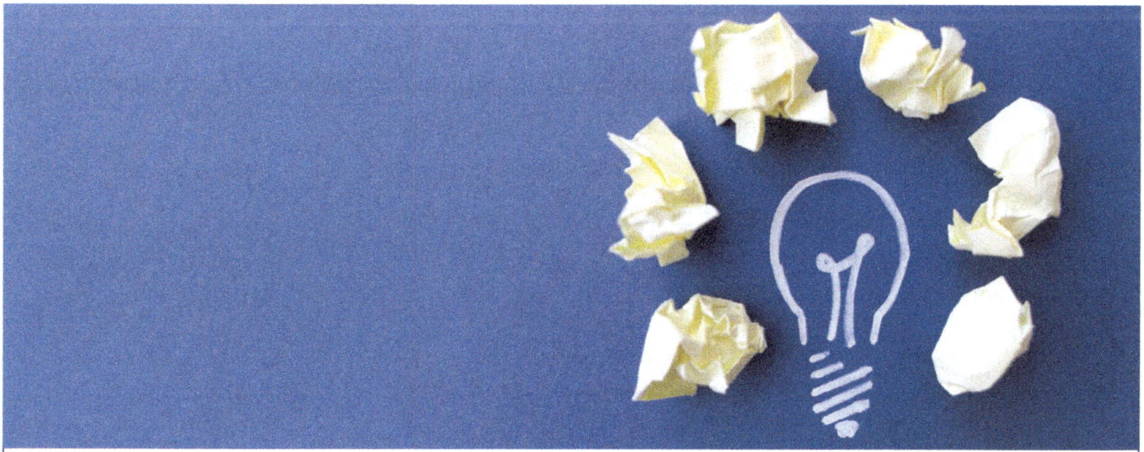

Let's embark on an exciting journey! You've already pinned down your specific niche and researched the competition - fantastic work. It's time to roll up your sleeves and bring your business idea to life.

This stage is all about finding a gap, a certain need, or a problem lurking within your chosen niche that is desperately waiting for a solution - your solution.

Let's get to work!

You have an idea for your niche, which is interesting, and you also figured out a business model, such as affiliate marketing, dropshipping, or publishing, that would generate constant revenue for your online business.

Now, it's time to turn the focus on the other players. Dig up everything on any other online companies or solo entrepreneurs who are offering the same service or products as you will.

The chances are high that you will bump into a bunch of future competitors, where the best scenario is ending up with a few big names who are doing something similar. Why? Because it proves that your idea is already working - only it's making others successful at the moment and not you. Don't get nervous about discovering that your idea is already out there.

In these cases, you can either get back to the first point and think of another one (not the easiest thing) or alter your present idea so that it can offer something better, faster, cheaper, and easier compared to your future competitors.

Also, if it seems like there are hundreds of others doing the same as you are planning to, don't simply just give up on your idea, but start thinking about how you could make it unique, you could take a product and market it to a different audience, for example.

Surely, if there are hundreds like you, they were able to do the same, so why give up? The next point might come in handy in this case.

Analyze and Learn

Gather every detail that you can on your future competitors. Know them and know them well. If you are going to join the competition for online success, it is vital to know the business model of the others.

How do they generate revenue? Who is the most successful? What are their strengths and weaknesses? What is their target audience? It might take considerable time, but these insights are vital in the long run.

Why? Because this can help you create value and transform your idea into an actual piece of art, that offers better capabilities compared to others. Furthermore, it helps you to make your future product or service UNIQUE!

If you have done your homework, you should be aware of the similar services or products out there. The information can help you to hone your future product or service and make it more unique.

All the data that you have gathered will get you vital insights into your target audience, the best business models out there, the various pricing possibilities, and the unique functions, services, or extras that are needed to differentiate your own service from your competitors. This is your way to uniqueness.

Branding

You have to look at your online business as a brand. The previous points can help you identify your message, and with a powerful message comes a strong brand. Think of the various aspects of branding strategies, from the smallest ones (picking the colors and fonts of your web page) to the more complex challenges (creating a logo or slogan).

You might consider talking to a professional who can help you create your brand identity, making connecting to your target audience easier. Once again, thorough research is indispensable and don't stop until at least you have a few good sketches or names.

Online Foundation

With all of these at hand, you should be ready to create the core of your online business, which consists of a well-designed and attractive website, an email address, and social media profiles.

You can set these up basically without launching the whole project, which gives you some buffer time to ensure that everything will go smoothly. Designing your website should be your top priority, as it will be your main tool to convert your readers/users/visitors into potential customers/subscribers.

Testing - Prelaunch

With every action step, you get closer to launching your online business; however, it also means that more and more issues or questions arise. To avoid a sloppy launch, it is advisable to run a testing phase, which can give you some extra time to deliver those final touches that are still missing. Get friends, colleagues, and ex-colleagues together and run a short test.

This will give you some initial insights on how could be your customer experience improved. In some cases, especially if you are planning to offer a service for other businesses, it might be advisable to have a few of your potential future customers join your initial test phase - offer them something in exchange, such as lower monthly fees for a year, which can easily get you your first customers together with invaluable insights.

On the other hand, you can also get your first testimonials, social followers, and email subscribers, so the initial testing can be your first milestone. You don't have to have your website domain or your business name yet. This can be part of how you refine your official launch through this testing phase.

Analyze and Implement

If your test phase seems to be 100% positive, the participants weren't honest, probably. At least you should be receiving a few remarks on the colors of the buttons on your homepage, or that your background image is not "that" cool, or that your "About us" page is glitchy. These test phases get you valuable feedback and even if you are 100% sure that everything is perfect, it is usually not.

Analyze the feedback you have received and implement any additional functions or changes that are recommended by the bigger percentage. Obviously, you won't be able to offer a product that fits everyone's needs, but you should be paying attention to the needs of your future audience.

Don't be upset if you run into a bunch of negative comments or weird suggestions. Remember that there is a possibility that one of them is a real game-changer. Don't get sloppy and spend time evaluating your new data.

CHAPTER 3 HOMEWORK

Let's Go Detective

Spot the voids or demands within your niche. Network with people involved in your niche and ask them about the pain points or inconveniences they face. Or organize surveys and market research? It's all about understanding what's missing and what needs fixing in your chosen field.

Is It a Go? Let's Find Out

You've got your solution, but how do we know it's a winner? It's time to validate your business idea through market research and testing. This might include gathering early feedback or running surveys to gauge its potential success.

Put On Your Creative Hat

Once you've figured out the puzzle, it's time to come up with a winning solution. Put your knowledge, your skills, and your unique expertise to good use. Create a product or a service that is set to transform and address these needs, offering a resolution to the problem you've identified.

Task Checklist

- [ ] I have developed a potential product or service
- [ ] I have unearthed the problems or needs within the niche
- [ ] I have validated my business idea through research and feedback

CHAPTER 4
BUSINESS PLAN

Your business plan should include your aspirations, the strategies to reach them, your business's structure, and the details surrounding the product or service you're offering.

1

Your Business Concept

Let's begin by painting a vivid picture of your business. What's the heart and soul of your enterprise? Which products or services are you passionately providing, and how are these making a positive difference in the lives of your customers?

2

Your Target Audience

It's time to zoom in on your customers. Can you describe them? What are their unique traits, their hopes, and their needs? How does your product or service step in to resolve the issues they face in their day-to-day lives?

3

Marketing & Sales Strategy

So, how do we get your brilliant solution into the hands of those who need it? Brainstorm on how you'll charm your customers and keep them coming back for more. What avenues will you explore to connect with them?

4

Day-To Day Operations

Let's switch gears and ponder on the inner workings of your business. How will the daily grind look? What tools, resources, and equipment will your business rely on? If you're delivering a tangible product, how will your supply chain function smoothly?

5

Your Financial Forecast

Now, let's delve into the numbers. Starting and running a business requires an investment, so how much are we talking about here? When do you envision your venture reaching that all-important break-even point and stepping into profitability?

Business Plan

THE EXECUTIVE SUMMARY

Worksheet

This should be completed LAST, even though it is first in your business plan.

This summarizes everything you have said in the other nine worksheets. Like an elevator pitch, if you were to try to explain your business in a minute or less, what would you say? It should be short, unique, interesting, and persuasive.

Business Plan

BUSINESS OVERVIEW

Worksheet

Write a detailed description of your business including the following elements:

The Legal Structure

- ☐ **Sole proprietor**
- ☐ **Partnership**
- ☐ **Corporation**
- ☐ **Limited Liability Corporation (LLC)**

Why have you selected this form of business?

Business Formation History
Mission Statement (Explain your reason for being and your guiding principles.)

Company Goals and Objectives
(Describe what you intend the business to achieve regarding the industry, customers, and even the world.)

Business Philosophy (What is important to the business and why?)

Customer Description
(To whom will you market your products/services?).

Industry Description
(Describe the expected growth and how your business can help.)

Business Strengths
(What factors will make the company succeed? What background experience, skills, and strengths give you an advantage over others?)

Location

State/Province:______________________________

Country:_________________________

Language:_________________________

Doing Business Via

Check or insert other options that apply to your business.

___ Website
___ Storefront
___ Online Shop
___ Email
___ Events
___ Home Shows
___ Online Advertising
___ Consignment Shops
___ Local Pickup/Delivery
___ News Subscription
___ FB Marketplace
___ Amazon
___ Sellwire
___ Etsy
___ _____________________
___ _____________________
___ _____________________
___ _____________________
___ _____________________
___ _____________________
___ _____________________

Business Plan

OPERATIONS PLAN

Worksheet

Explain and describe how each business area will function. Include info about the physical setup and the responsibilities for specific tasks that team members will perform. These tasks/procedures are called Standard Operating Procedures (SOP).

Business Area: ______________________________

Task: ______________ Subject/Issue: ______________

Team/Members: ______________________________

SOP: ______________________________

____

____

____

____

____

____

____

____

____

____

Explain and describe how each business area will function. Include info about the physical setup and the responsibilities for specific tasks that team members will perform. These tasks/procedures are called Standard Operating Procedures (SOP).

Business Area: ______________________________

Task: ______________ Subject/Issue: ______________

Team/Members: ______________________________

SOP: ______________________________

____

____

____

____

____

Business Area: ______________________________

Task: ______________ Subject/Issue: ______________

Team/Members: ______________________________

SOP: ______________________________

____

____

____

____

____

Business Area: ______________________________

Task: ____________________ Subject/Issue: ____________________

Team/Members: ______________________________

SOP: ______________________________

____

____

____

____

____

Business Area: ______________________________

Task: ____________________ Subject/Issue: ____________________

Team/Members: ______________________________

SOP: ______________________________

____

____

____

____

____

Business Area: ______________________________

Task: ______________ Subject/Issue: ______________

Team/Members: ______________________________

SOP: ______________________________

____

____

____

____

____

Business Area: ______________________________

Task: ______________ Subject/Issue: ______________

Team/Members: ______________________________

SOP: ______________________________

____

____

____

____

____

Describe and explain how you intend to meet the wants and needs of your market.

Business Plan

PRODUCTS & SERVICES

Worksheet

Describe the products you create, sell, and/or the services you offer. Use the following list to help you discover new ideas and identify and classify your products or services. Then, provide a brief description of each existing product.

Writing/Publishing/Ebooks

____ Ebook – non-fiction
____ Ebook – fiction
____ Poetry book
____ Ecommerce product descriptions
____ Copywriting templates
____ Recipe books
____ Document templates
____ Reports/analytics templates
____ Email campaign templates
____ Academic research, papers, findings
____ Magazines
____ Writing cover letters
____ ______________________________
____ ______________________________
____ ______________________________

Audio

____ Songs
____ Beats
____ Jingles
____ Ringtones
____ Sound effects
____ Voice overs (as a service)
____ Instrumental tracks
____ ______________________________
____ ______________________________
____ ______________________________

Video

____ Sell short films (entertainment)
____ Video animation intros
____ Stock video
____ Video tutorials (ex. How tos)
____ Professionally edited event videos as a service
____ Documentary
____ Stand-up comedy
____ YouTuber
____ ______________________________
____ ______________________________
____ ______________________________

Design

____ Wallpapers
____ Posters/prints
____ Emojis/bitmojis
____ Fonts
____ Photoshop/illustrator templates
____ Branding services
____ Photoshop services (airbrushing, touch ups, etc.)
____ Logo design
____ Business card design
____ Infographic design
____ Turn images into vector files
____ PowerPoints / Keynote presentation templates
____ Printable coloring book pages
____ 3D models
____ VR/AR templates
____ Icon sets
____ Wedding invitation templates
____ Comics
____ Printable calendars
____ Printable journals
____ Clipart / AI-generated images
____ Tumbler designs / craft templates
____ ______________________________
____ ______________________________
____ ______________________________

Photography

____ Lightroom/photoshop presets
____ Mockup images
____ Stock photos
____ LUTs (Lookup Tables)
____ Professionally edited event videos as a service
____ Documentary
____ Stand-up comedy
____ YouTuber
____ Influencer
____ ______________________________
____ ______________________________
____ ______________________________

IT/Tech

____ Apps
____ Games
____ Browser plugins
____ Website themes / Shopify themes
____ Setup for online stores, blogs, websites
____ Selling domains
____ Provide hosting reseller services
____ Zapier templates
____ Code snippets
____ Wordpress templates
____ ______________________________
____ ______________________________
____ ______________________________

Teaching & Skill Sharing

____ Language Lessons
____ Financial Consultations
____ Financial Planning
____ Coaching/mentoring sessions
____ Tutoring

____ Resume' touchup services
____ Essay writing service
____ Translations
____ Social media marketing
____ User testing
____ Proofreading service
____ Editing
____ Audits (accounting audits, content audits, etc.)
____ Career consultations
____ Virtual assisting
____ ______________________________
____ ______________________________
____ ______________________________

How-Tos & Digital Courses

____ Courses – of any and all kinds
____ Sewing patterns
____ Knitting patterns
____ Nutrition plans
____ Meal-prep plans
____ Workout plans
____ Worksheets (educational curriculum ideas)
____ Paid newsletters
____ Woodworking instructions – step-by-step tutorials
____ Board game printouts
____ Meditation/subliminal programs
____ Painting tutorials
____ ______________________________
____ ______________________________
____ ______________________________

Your Products and Services

Product/Service Name: ______________________________
Category: ______________________________
Format/Type (eBook, audio, etc.): ______________________________
Description: ______________________________
____
____

Product/Service Name: ______________________________
Category: ______________________________
Format/Type (eBook, audio, etc.): ______________________________
Description: ______________________________
____
____

Product/Service Name: ______________________________
Category: ______________________________
Format/Type (eBook, audio, etc.): ______________________________
Description: ______________________________
____
____

Product/Service Name: ______________________________
Category: ______________________________
Format/Type (eBook, audio, etc.): ______________________________
Description: ______________________________
____
____

Product/Service Name: ______________________________
Category: ______________________________
Format/Type (eBook, audio, etc.): ______________________________
Description: ______________________________
____
____

Product/Service Name: ______________________________
Category: ______________________________
Format/Type (eBook, audio, etc.): ______________________________
Description: ______________________________
____
____

Business Plan

SALES & MARKETING

Worksheet

Fill in the following information to help you make sales and market your items/services.

Product/Service Name:____
Description:____
____

What customer needs does this product fill or what issues does it solve?

____________________________ ____________________________

____________________________ ____________________________

Price:______________________ Sale Price: ____________________

How do these prices compare to your competitors' prices?

____

____

What motivation prompts potential buyers to take action and make the purchase?

____________________________ ____________________________

____________________________ ____________________________

____________________________ ____________________________

What methods will you use to market this product/service?

____

Where and how will you "advertise" or notify potential customers of this specific offer?

____

____

____

Draft a potential ad for this product/service:

____

____

More Promotion Ideas for This Offer

Ad 2 for this product/service:

____

____

____

____

Ad 3 for this product/service:

____

____

____

____

Ad 4 for this product/service:

____

____

____

____

Additional Promotion Ideas

____

____

____

____

____

____

____

____

____

____

____

____

____

Business Plan

COMPETITIVE ANALYSIS

Worksheet

On this worksheet, you will identify and research your competitors to assess your direct and indirect competitors' strengths and weaknesses to compare to your own.

Factor	Me	Competitor 1	Competitor 2	Importance Rate
Products	Strong / Weak	Strong / Weak	Strong / Weak	1 2 3 4 5
Price	Strong / Weak	Strong / Weak	Strong / Weak	1 2 3 4 5
Quality	Strong / Weak	Strong / Weak	Strong / Weak	1 2 3 4 5
Selection	Strong / Weak	Strong / Weak	Strong / Weak	1 2 3 4 5
Service	Strong / Weak	Strong / Weak	Strong / Weak	1 2 3 4 5
Reliability	Strong / Weak	Strong / Weak	Strong / Weak	1 2 3 4 5
Stability	Strong / Weak	Strong / Weak	Strong / Weak	1 2 3 4 5
Expertise	Strong / Weak	Strong / Weak	Strong / Weak	1 2 3 4 5
Reputation	Strong / Weak	Strong / Weak	Strong / Weak	1 2 3 4 5
Location	Strong / Weak	Strong / Weak	Strong / Weak	1 2 3 4 5
Appearance	Strong / Weak	Strong / Weak	Strong / Weak	1 2 3 4 5
Sale Method	Strong / Weak	Strong / Weak	Strong / Weak	1 2 3 4 5
Credit Policy	Strong / Weak	Strong / Weak	Strong / Weak	1 2 3 4 5
Advertising	Strong / Weak	Strong / Weak	Strong / Weak	1 2 3 4 5
Images	Strong / Weak	Strong / Weak	Strong / Weak	1 2 3 4 5
___________	Strong / Weak	Strong / Weak	Strong / Weak	1 2 3 4 5
___________	Strong / Weak	Strong / Weak	Strong / Weak	1 2 3 4 5
___________	Strong / Weak	Strong / Weak	Strong / Weak	1 2 3 4 5
___________	Strong / Weak	Strong / Weak	Strong / Weak	1 2 3 4 5

Describe how you can develop a competitive advantage over your competition using the information you discovered when you did your research and analysis.

Business Plan

MANAGEMENT TEAM

Worksheet

Provide pertinent, concise background information on all key players involved in the business.

Business Area:________________________ Team ______________________________
Name:______________________________________

Business/Job Info

Profession:_____________________________________
Specialty:______________________________________
Website:____
Referred by:____________________________________ Date:_____________________

Rating: _____________________________________

Skills:

____________________________________ ____________________________________
____________________________________ ____________________________________
____________________________________ ____________________________________
____________________________________ ____________________________________

Interests:

____________________________________ ____________________________________
____________________________________ ____________________________________
____________________________________ ____________________________________
____________________________________ ____________________________________

Other:____
____

Personal Info

Mailing Address: ____
____
Email: ____
Phone 1 #: _______________________________________
Phone 2 #: _______________________________________

Business Area:______________________ Team ___________________________
Name:___________________________________

Business/Job Info

Profession:__________________________________
Specialty:___________________________________
Website:____________________________________
Referred by:_________________________________ Date:___________________

Rating: __________________________________

Skills:

________________________________ ________________________________
________________________________ ________________________________
________________________________ ________________________________
________________________________ ________________________________

Interests:

________________________________ ________________________________
________________________________ ________________________________
________________________________ ________________________________
________________________________ ________________________________

Other:____
____

Personal Info

Mailing Address: ____
____
Email: ____
Phone 1 #: ___________________________________
Phone 2 #: ___________________________________

Business Area:______________________ Team ___________________________
Name:___________________________________

Business/Job Info
Profession:___________________________________
Specialty:_____________________________________
Website:______________________________________
Referred by:__________________________________ Date:___________________

Rating: ___________________________________

Skills:

________________________________ ________________________________
________________________________ ________________________________
________________________________ ________________________________
________________________________ ________________________________

Interests:

________________________________ ________________________________
________________________________ ________________________________
________________________________ ________________________________
________________________________ ________________________________

Other:____
____

Personal Info
Mailing Address: ____
____
Email: ____
Phone 1 #: _____________________________________
Phone 2 #: _____________________________________

Business Area:_______________________ Team ____________________________
Name:_____________________________________

Business/Job Info
Profession:____________________________________
Specialty:_____________________________________
Website:______________________________________
Referred by:___________________________________ Date:____________________

Rating: ____________________________________

Skills:

__________________________________ __________________________________
__________________________________ __________________________________
__________________________________ __________________________________
__________________________________ __________________________________

Interests:

__________________________________ __________________________________
__________________________________ __________________________________
__________________________________ __________________________________
__________________________________ __________________________________

Other:____
____

Personal Info
Mailing Address: ____
____
Email: ____
Phone 1 #: ______________________________________
Phone 2 #: ______________________________________

Business Area:____________________ Team ________________________
Name:________________________________

Business/Job Info

Profession:_______________________________
Specialty:________________________________
Website:_________________________________
Referred by:______________________________ Date:_________________

Rating: _______________________________

Skills:

Interests:

Other:____

Personal Info

Mailing Address: ____

Email: ____
Phone 1 #: _______________________________
Phone 2 #: _______________________________

Business Plan

FINANCIAL PLAN

Worksheet

Include all financial information for each section below.

Amount needed to start the business includes:

Item: ________________________________ Cost: ______________
Item: ________________________________ Cost: ______________
Item: ________________________________ Cost: ______________
Item: ________________________________ Cost: ______________
Item: ________________________________ Cost: ______________
Item: ________________________________ Cost: ______________
Item: ________________________________ Cost: ______________
Item: ________________________________ Cost: ______________
Item: ________________________________ Cost: ______________
Item: ________________________________ Cost: ______________
Item: ________________________________ Cost: ______________
Item: ________________________________ Cost: ______________
Item: ________________________________ Cost: ______________
Item: ________________________________ Cost: ______________
Item: ________________________________ Cost: ______________
Item: ________________________________ Cost: ______________
Item: ________________________________ Cost: ______________
Item: ________________________________ Cost: ______________
Item: ________________________________ Cost: ______________
Item: ________________________________ Cost: ______________
Item: ________________________________ Cost: ______________
Item: ________________________________ Cost: ______________
Item: ________________________________ Cost: ______________
Item: ________________________________ Cost: ______________
Item: ________________________________ Cost: ______________
Item: ________________________________ Cost: ______________
Item: ________________________________ Cost: ______________

Total Cost: __________________

Amount needed to maintain the business for the first year includes:

Item: ______________________________ Cost: ____________
Item: ______________________________ Cost: ____________
Item: ______________________________ Cost: ____________
Item: ______________________________ Cost: ____________
Item: ______________________________ Cost: ____________
Item: ______________________________ Cost: ____________
Item: ______________________________ Cost: ____________
Item: ______________________________ Cost: ____________
Item: ______________________________ Cost: ____________
Item: ______________________________ Cost: ____________
Item: ______________________________ Cost: ____________
Item: ______________________________ Cost: ____________
Item: ______________________________ Cost: ____________
Item: ______________________________ Cost: ____________
Item: ______________________________ Cost: ____________
Item: ______________________________ Cost: ____________
Item: ______________________________ Cost: ____________
Item: ______________________________ Cost: ____________
Item: ______________________________ Cost: ____________
Item: ______________________________ Cost: ____________
Item: ______________________________ Cost: ____________
Item: ______________________________ Cost: ____________
Item: ______________________________ Cost: ____________
Item: ______________________________ Cost: ____________
Item: ______________________________ Cost: ____________
Item: ______________________________ Cost: ____________
Item: ______________________________ Cost: ____________
Item: ______________________________ Cost: ____________
Item: ______________________________ Cost: ____________
Item: ______________________________ Cost: ____________
Item: ______________________________ Cost: ____________
Item: ______________________________ Cost: ____________
Item: ______________________________ Cost: ____________

Total Cost: ________________

Amount needed for the first two years includes:

Item: ________________________ Cost: ____________
Item: ________________________ Cost: ____________
Item: ________________________ Cost: ____________
Item: ________________________ Cost: ____________
Item: ________________________ Cost: ____________
Item: ________________________ Cost: ____________
Item: ________________________ Cost: ____________
Item: ________________________ Cost: ____________
Item: ________________________ Cost: ____________
Item: ________________________ Cost: ____________
Item: ________________________ Cost: ____________
Item: ________________________ Cost: ____________
Item: ________________________ Cost: ____________
Item: ________________________ Cost: ____________
Item: ________________________ Cost: ____________
Item: ________________________ Cost: ____________
Item: ________________________ Cost: ____________
Item: ________________________ Cost: ____________
Item: ________________________ Cost: ____________
Item: ________________________ Cost: ____________
Item: ________________________ Cost: ____________
Item: ________________________ Cost: ____________
Item: ________________________ Cost: ____________
Item: ________________________ Cost: ____________
Item: ________________________ Cost: ____________
Item: ________________________ Cost: ____________
Item: ________________________ Cost: ____________
Item: ________________________ Cost: ____________
Item: ________________________ Cost: ____________
Item: ________________________ Cost: ____________
Item: ________________________ Cost: ____________
Item: ________________________ Cost: ____________
Item: ________________________ Cost: ____________

Total Cost: ________________

Amount needed for three years includes:

Item: ______________________________ Cost: ____________
Item: ______________________________ Cost: ____________
Item: ______________________________ Cost: ____________
Item: ______________________________ Cost: ____________
Item: ______________________________ Cost: ____________
Item: ______________________________ Cost: ____________
Item: ______________________________ Cost: ____________
Item: ______________________________ Cost: ____________
Item: ______________________________ Cost: ____________
Item: ______________________________ Cost: ____________
Item: ______________________________ Cost: ____________
Item: ______________________________ Cost: ____________
Item: ______________________________ Cost: ____________
Item: ______________________________ Cost: ____________
Item: ______________________________ Cost: ____________
Item: ______________________________ Cost: ____________
Item: ______________________________ Cost: ____________
Item: ______________________________ Cost: ____________
Item: ______________________________ Cost: ____________
Item: ______________________________ Cost: ____________
Item: ______________________________ Cost: ____________
Item: ______________________________ Cost: ____________
Item: ______________________________ Cost: ____________
Item: ______________________________ Cost: ____________
Item: ______________________________ Cost: ____________
Item: ______________________________ Cost: ____________
Item: ______________________________ Cost: ____________
Item: ______________________________ Cost: ____________
Item: ______________________________ Cost: ____________
Item: ______________________________ Cost: ____________
Item: ______________________________ Cost: ____________
Item: ______________________________ Cost: ____________
Item: ______________________________ Cost: ____________

Total Cost: ________________

Amount needed for five years includes:

Item: ______________________________ Cost: ____________
Item: ______________________________ Cost: ____________
Item: ______________________________ Cost: ____________
Item: ______________________________ Cost: ____________
Item: ______________________________ Cost: ____________
Item: ______________________________ Cost: ____________
Item: ______________________________ Cost: ____________
Item: ______________________________ Cost: ____________
Item: ______________________________ Cost: ____________
Item: ______________________________ Cost: ____________
Item: ______________________________ Cost: ____________
Item: ______________________________ Cost: ____________
Item: ______________________________ Cost: ____________
Item: ______________________________ Cost: ____________
Item: ______________________________ Cost: ____________
Item: ______________________________ Cost: ____________
Item: ______________________________ Cost: ____________
Item: ______________________________ Cost: ____________
Item: ______________________________ Cost: ____________
Item: ______________________________ Cost: ____________
Item: ______________________________ Cost: ____________
Item: ______________________________ Cost: ____________
Item: ______________________________ Cost: ____________
Item: ______________________________ Cost: ____________
Item: ______________________________ Cost: ____________
Item: ______________________________ Cost: ____________
Item: ______________________________ Cost: ____________
Item: ______________________________ Cost: ____________
Item: ______________________________ Cost: ____________
Item: ______________________________ Cost: ____________
Item: ______________________________ Cost: ____________
Item: ______________________________ Cost: ____________
Item: ______________________________ Cost: ____________

Total Cost: ________________

Plans to use funds

Anticipated need for additional funding for these items:

Item: ______________________________ Cost: ____________
Item: ______________________________ Cost: ____________
Item: ______________________________ Cost: ____________
Item: ______________________________ Cost: ____________
Item: ______________________________ Cost: ____________
Item: ______________________________ Cost: ____________
Item: ______________________________ Cost: ____________
Item: ______________________________ Cost: ____________
Item: ______________________________ Cost: ____________
Item: ______________________________ Cost: ____________
Item: ______________________________ Cost: ____________
Item: ______________________________ Cost: ____________
Item: ______________________________ Cost: ____________
Item: ______________________________ Cost: ____________
Item: ______________________________ Cost: ____________
Item: ______________________________ Cost: ____________
Item: ______________________________ Cost: ____________
Item: ______________________________ Cost: ____________
Item: ______________________________ Cost: ____________
Item: ______________________________ Cost: ____________
Item: ______________________________ Cost: ____________
Item: ______________________________ Cost: ____________
Item: ______________________________ Cost: ____________
Item: ______________________________ Cost: ____________
Item: ______________________________ Cost: ____________
Item: ______________________________ Cost: ____________
Item: ______________________________ Cost: ____________
Item: ______________________________ Cost: ____________
Item: ______________________________ Cost: ____________
Item: ______________________________ Cost: ____________
Item: ______________________________ Cost: ____________
Item: ______________________________ Cost: ____________
Item: ______________________________ Cost: ____________

Total Cost: ________________

Ongoing business expenses/subscriptions includes:

Item: ________________________________ Cost: ______________
Item: ________________________________ Cost: ______________
Item: ________________________________ Cost: ______________
Item: ________________________________ Cost: ______________
Item: ________________________________ Cost: ______________
Item: ________________________________ Cost: ______________
Item: ________________________________ Cost: ______________
Item: ________________________________ Cost: ______________
Item: ________________________________ Cost: ______________
Item: ________________________________ Cost: ______________
Item: ________________________________ Cost: ______________
Item: ________________________________ Cost: ______________
Item: ________________________________ Cost: ______________
Item: ________________________________ Cost: ______________
Item: ________________________________ Cost: ______________
Item: ________________________________ Cost: ______________
Item: ________________________________ Cost: ______________
Item: ________________________________ Cost: ______________
Item: ________________________________ Cost: ______________
Item: ________________________________ Cost: ______________
Item: ________________________________ Cost: ______________
Item: ________________________________ Cost: ______________
Item: ________________________________ Cost: ______________
Item: ________________________________ Cost: ______________
Item: ________________________________ Cost: ______________
Item: ________________________________ Cost: ______________
Item: ________________________________ Cost: ______________
Item: ________________________________ Cost: ______________
Item: ________________________________ Cost: ______________
Item: ________________________________ Cost: ______________
Item: ________________________________ Cost: ______________
Item: ________________________________ Cost: ______________
Item: ________________________________ Cost: ______________

Total Cost: ________________

Projected Income Statement Worksheet for: ______________________________

from ____________ to ____________

Months	1	2	3	4	5	6	7	8	9	10	11	12
Total Revenue												
Cost of Goods Sold Services Provided												
Gross Profit												
Admin Salaries												
Rent/Mortgage												
Business Equipment												
Outsourcing Bills												
Marketing/Advertising												
Accounting & Legal												
Office Space												
Travel												
Vehicles												
Depreciation												
Repairs & Maintenance												
Licenses												
Taxes-Payroll												
Taxes-Other												
Phone												
Business Subscriptions												
Utilities												
Office Supplies												
Interest												
Postage												
Miscellaneous												
Other:												
Total Expenses												
Pre-Tax Profit (Loss)												

Business Plan

YOUR NOTES

This space is yours to make draft notes for your business plan.

Business Plan

YOUR NOTES

This space is yours to make draft notes for your business plan.

Business Plan

YOUR NOTES

This space is yours to make draft notes for your business plan.

Business Plan

YOUR NOTES

This space is yours to make draft notes for your business plan.

CHAPTER 5 BUILDING YOUR WEBSITE

Think of your website as the virtual counterpart of a bustling, lively, and engaging brick-and-mortar shop.

1

Choose Your Name

Choose a domain name that truly reflects what your brand is about and stands out. Next, secure web hosting services that can cater to your business' unique needs.

2

Start Designing

Aim for an aesthetic that's not only visually engaging but allows customers to navigate around easily. Keep it cohesive with your brand, making sure the colors, fonts, and imagery all echo your identity.

3

Bring Your Design To Life

Developing your website involves behind-the-scenes work to make your beautiful design functional. If tech isn't your strongest suit, consider enlisting the help of a professional web developer.

4

Online Checkout

If you plan to sell your products or services online, you'll need to equip your site with e-commerce capabilities such as an online shopping cart.

5

Put It To The Test

Finally, make sure to test your website thoroughly. Just like how you'd do a dry run before the grand opening of a physical store, you need to ensure all features work flawlessly and the customer journey is smooth.

CHOOSE YOUR NAME

Your business name is highly likely to also be your website name, which is highly likely to also be your domain name.

Choosing Your Name & Domain Name

In preparing to launch a new website, there are several things you will need to do before you can even begin to think about content writing or SEO.

Of course, one of the most fundamental starting points is to find a hosting service and to choose a domain name for your site or blog.

This will give you somewhere to store the files that make up your site and give your visitors a way to access them.

But deciding on a domain name is more than just a practical matter; it's also going to have a huge impact on how your visitors view your site and how you'll promote it.

Here, we'll look at how to choose a domain name that will make sense from a business standpoint and a creative one.

Branding

Coming up with a name for your website that you can build a brand around makes much sense for several reasons. For one, Google has explicitly stated that it will try to give more prominence to brands and bury 'exact name domains' (keyword URLs) to show better quality sites.

At the same time, though, creating a brand name will give you more opportunity for future expansion, meaning that you can more easily market your site and create awareness while using that same branding in your advertising.

Memorability

Of course, if you want people to come to your site often and spread the word, then choosing a URL that will be easy to remember also makes sense.

If your website name is too long or nonsensical, then this will mean that people struggle to go to your site or tell others about it. Too long means anything longer than 16 characters between the dots.

Do not use dashes and underscores; make the URL as catchy as possible.

ALWAYS get the ".com." If your domain name is unavailable as the ".com," then choose a different domain name. Yes, it's that important. Do not settle for the .net, .org, etc.

Do not use any numerals or numbers, only letters, which includes not spelling out a number.

Say it out loud to ensure it does not "trip" over the tongue when speaking it. The domain name needs to be easily and smoothly spoken. It makes it easier for others to talk about it.

Make it easily spelled when heard. The last thing you want is to make people have to spell your domain name every time they are talking about it. Potential customers will have difficulty finding your site if it is not easy to spell.

Uniqueness

Coming up with a name for your website that you can build a brand around makes much sense for several reasons. For one, Google has explicitly stated that it will try to give more prominence to brands and bury 'exact name domains' (keyword URLs) to show better quality sites.

At the same time, though, creating a brand name will give you more opportunity for future expansion, meaning that you can more easily market your site and create awareness while using that same branding in your advertising.

Other Considerations

Besides these points, there are many more considerations to keep in mind, though the degree to which they apply to your site will vary.

For instance, if your business is likely to be listed alphabetically, coming up with a URL beginning with 'A' or even '1' could be a good way to get yourself near the top.

Also, you may also want to consider the length of your domain, and of course, this is all just academic until you consider the price and availability.

Top Tip: While you don't necessarily need to buy the trademark for your domain name, it is a good idea to ensure that nobody else has already bought it.

Check that there are no websites that have very similar names, and likewise, do a search for trademarks to make sure that the name you want is not trademarked (https://www.uspto.gov/trademark).

CHOOSE HOSTING

Your business name is highly likely to also be your website name, which is highly likely to also be your domain name.

Now you have a name for your website, the next step is to build it. This means doing a few things:

- Investing in a web host
- Buying your domain name
- Creating the basic foundation of your website

A web host is where your site will be stored. Popular options include:

Bluehost, Godaddy, Hostgator, Wix and Shopify

Bluehost, Godaddy, and Hostgator are more for informational sites, services, or blogging. You would typically install and use WordPress on these sites. I would not recommend GoDaddy, though. They have a different version of WordPress and are very limited in options.

Wix and Shopify are for e-commerce stores where you would sell products. This is where you could use dropshipping or print on demand, or possibly a hybrid of the two, as your business model.

A web host provides you with space on a huge, always-connected computer called a server. You upload the files that constitute your website to this computer, and then when someone types your URL into the address bar, they will be shown those files.

That's why you, of course, also need to buy the domain name. You can do this separately, but the good news is that most web hosts will also allow you to buy a domain name through their site directly. Once you click that you want to sign up, this will be the first thing you do before you pay for a deal.

CHAPTER 5 HOMEWORK

Chose your domain and dependable hosting service

☐

Completed a stylish and user-friendly website design

☐

Wrapped up website development

☐

Installed ecommerce; ready to process transactions

☐

Tested to guarantee a seamless user experience

☐

CHAPTER 6
UNDERSTAND SEO

SEO is about bringing a steady stream of potential customers right to your digital doorstep. There is so much to understand about SEO that it deserves its own book. I will not go into extreme detail about SEO because you can find information online to learn SEO. I will give you the basics.

☐ Understanding the basics of SEO

It's a bit like learning a new language, but instead of conversing with people, you're communicating with search engines. Take the time to research how search engines work and how they rank websites.

☐ Successfully identify relevant keywords

What are the magic words that make your potential customers tick, the phrases they punch into their search bar when they're looking for the products or services you provide? Spend time identifying these.

☐ Implement SEO strategies

Picture on-page SEO as the inner workings of your website, optimizing everything in your content. Off-page SEO is all about external influences that boost your site in search engines' eyes.

☐ Monitoring and adjusting SEO results

Utilize powerful tools like Google Analytics to gauge your website's performance of search engine results. If something's not working as well as it should, don't worry - this allows you to tweak and refine your strategies.

SEO BASICS

Traffic is the prerequisite for any successful business. Like a typical brick-and-mortar shop that needs people walking around to see their shop, an online business also needs eyeballs. The problem is that many new entrepreneurs need a bigger financial budget or know how to generate tons of business traffic. Then, in the early internet marketing years, a group of people coined the term "SEO Marketing," which has been at the forefront of free traffic generation. Let's delve deeper into this amazing phenomenon.

The Beginnings

One of the good things about SEO marketing is that it can create passive traffic. This means you'll be getting traffic without having to be there actively. This seems like the ultimate choice, especially for marketers on a shoestring budget.

The essence of SEO marketing is that traffic generation relies on optimizing web content to draw free traffic through search engines such as the big "G" (Google).

Google is the biggest search engine in the world, with millions of searches going on daily. By tapping into SEO, you can be swimming in loads of traffic. SEO is the art of getting your page high in Google's search results for search terms relevant to your online niche business.

Let's say you are in the dog training niche. Hence, when people search for terms like "dog training tips" or "dog training guide," you want your web page to appear on the first page of the search results – And that is what SEO is all about.

The better you are at SEO, the more traffic and sales you will get. Of course, if you have a huge marketing budget, you can spend it all on advertising and totally forego SEO, but if you are on a shoestring budget, you can always tap into the powers of SEO to get tons of free traffic. SEO is slower than paid traffic. You will either spend your time, or you will spend money for results.

Keyword Research

The Research You will need to find what keywords are the most sought-after in your niche and target them in your web content. That way, when most people search for something on the net, everything will lead to your website.

The best place to do your keyword search is at Google Ads Tool, where you must create a free account at ads.google.com.

The winning formula for effective keywords is 1) High search volume and 2) Low competition. As a general rule of thumb, getting more than 1000 organic searches daily is a good bet for a highly searched keyword. If you want to check out your competition, get the Google toolbar and see what the "page ranks" for search results are on the first page of search results.

These keywords and key phrases will then be targeted to draw you massive free traffic via SEO. There are also long tail keywords with longer key phrases and 5 with less search volumes but virtually no competition. These should be targeted as well.

Website Optimization

There are two types of optimization techniques: Onsite optimization and Offsite optimization. Onsite optimization deals with the things you can tweak and modify on your website to make it more relevant to Google searches. Offsite optimization deals with interactions with websites outside of your own.

This could be in the form of getting backlinks or social interactions, which we will go into more detail later. The SEO trends are constantly evolving. That is because people are constantly exploiting SEO using "black hat" techniques that temporarily may put their websites on top of the search ranks. But Google is too smart to allow that for too long, and they have a team that constantly evolves Google's algorithm to ensure that searches remain relevant. The best techniques are considered "white hat," which you should follow.

Onsite Optimization

The first thing you must know is keywords. In short, every page should have about 2-5% keyword density. So sprinkle your keywords where they're due, but don't overdo it. For total optimization, keywords or key phrases should be present in the titles of your pages, the first sentence of the first paragraph, and at least once in the body.

Keywords should also be bolded or italicized now and then. Links should be worded with anchor text links (keywords and phrases).

Also, onsite linkages are highly recommended. You should link blog posts and pages together if they are relevant. These small steps contribute to SEO and should be applied when convenient. One more thing about on-site SEO: some say images don't contribute to SEO. I beg to differ. Images should be given alternate texts or descriptions. You can also link images to blog posts.

Stick to these good practices, and you'll be on your way to free organic traffic.

Offsite Optimization

A backlink is someone else's website linking to you. Pages with higher page rank that link back to you give more Google Juice. The key is to get as many high page rank as possible RELEVANT websites linking back to you. Quality over quantity, nuff said.

So, it would be a good idea to scout your competitors' websites and request a link exchange. Another important component is social interactions. As I said, Google's algorithm changes occasionally, and recently, they implemented a new ruling that social interactions are important for SEO.

This could be things like sharing on Facebook, Twitter, comments, etc. The world is connected everywhere now, not a stand-alone component.

CHAPTER 7 REGISTERING YOUR BUSINESS

Legally establishing your business offers the advantage of separating your personal assets from those of your enterprise, thereby protecting you from personal liability in the event of your business's debts. Moreover, it offers certain tax incentives and legal protections, such as securing your brand through trademark rights.

Choose your business entity type

This could be a sole proprietor, a partnership LLC, a corporation, etc. The structure will depend on your country's legal systems and what is most suitable for your business needs.

Register your business name

This name is what you will use on all official documents and applications, including your business tax ID application. Make sure you are happy with it!

Apply for a business tax ID

You'll need to get this number from your country's tax department. It's the unique identifier for your business in the tax world. In the US, this is the Federal EIN.

Necessary permits and licenses

The specifics of these will depend on what your business is, where it's located, and the rules of the game in your country or region. Do your research!

Register for regional and local taxes

Depending on your country's location, you may need to register with regional and local authorities for applicable taxes. In the US, this would be your state's tax ID number.

Homework

- [ ] Pick the perfect business entity type
- [ ] Business name—officially registered!
- [ ] Got your business tax ID
- [ ] Registration for regional and local taxes
- [ ] Secured necessary permits and licenses

CHAPTER 8 LEGAL CONSIDERATIONS

Understanding the legal aspect of running an online business is essential to avoid potential legal issues. These can range from copyright infringement and trademark issues to data security breaches and privacy violations. Let's go over a few below. It's important to consult with a business attorney, your local chamber of commerce, and an accountant for accurate legal and tax guidance.

- [ ] **Understand and comply with online business laws**

These could include e-commerce regulations, privacy laws, and data protection laws.

- [ ] **Create a privacy policy for your website**

This outlines how your business collects, uses, discloses, and manages a customer's data.

- [ ] **Develop terms of service for your business**

These are the legal agreements between a company and a user who wants to use that company's services.

- [ ] **Consider intellectual property protections**

Depending on your business, you might need trademarks, copyrights, or patents.

Get ready to promote your business and connect with your ideal customers.

CHAPTER 9
MARKETING YOUR BUSINESS

Effective marketing is a fundamental pillar that drives the successful growth of any business. It is the magnet that draws potential customers into the vicinity of your brand, sparking an initial interest that could possibly lead to a fruitful relationship.

The primary purpose of marketing is to reach out to consumers who may not be aware of the existence of your business or the value proposition it offers. It's about broadcasting your unique selling points, demonstrating the benefits, and showcasing your business's solutions. Doing so creates a strong presence in your industry, raises your visibility among potential clients, and sets you apart from your competition.

MARKETING TASKS

Start creating your business marketing plan

Identifying Suitable Marketing Channels

Find the best marketing channels for your business. These could range from search engine advertising to social media marketing. Email marketing is another effective channel. It's about discovering where your customers are and reaching out to them in a way that resonates with their needs and interests.

Developing a Marketing Content Strategy

Once you have identified the channels, the next task is to develop a compelling content strategy. What types of content will you create that will not only catch your audience's attention but also provoke them to engage with your brand? Do research and create a list.

Implement a Marketing Strategy

After you've devised your content strategy, it's time to bring it to life with marketing campaigns. These are purposeful efforts aligned with a specific message or goal, such as launching a new product, promoting a sale, or simply raising brand awareness. Plan your first campaign.

Adapting your Marketing Strategies

The final but important task is to monitor the results of your marketing efforts. Use analytical tools such as Google Analytics to track your progress. These signposts guide you, providing crucial insights that can help you refine your strategies as needed. It's about understanding what worked and what didn't and how to improve your next campaign.

CHAPTER 10

5-day

SOCIAL MEDIA CHALLENGE

Here's a suggested 5-day challenge to help you as a new online business owner become more comfortable with using social media to drive awareness and sales.

---

1. Review and update your social media profiles. Make sure you have a professional photo, a compelling bio, and links to your website or online shop. Use keywords related to your business in your bio to increase visibility.

2. Spend some time exploring social media for content related to your business. Look at what competitors are posting, what's getting engagement, and what might not be working as well.

3. Create a piece of original content related to your business. It could be a product photo, a behind-the-scenes video, a blog post, or a customer testimonial. Make sure it aligns with your brand and speaks to your target audience.

4. Engagement is a two-way street. Spend some time liking, commenting on, and sharing posts from other businesses or potential customers.

5. Create a simple social media content calendar for the next week. This could just be a list of what you plan to post each day. Remember to vary your content types (images, videos, articles, etc.) and include some engagement activities like asking questions or inviting comments.

MARKETING CHECKLIST

Check off marketing tasks and the social media challenge when completed!

- ◯ Identified Suitable Marketing Channels
- ◯ Developed a Marketing Content Strategy
- ◯ Implemented a Marketing Strategy
- ◯ Adapted your Marketing Strategies
- ◯ Reviewed and updated social media profiles
- ◯ Explored social media for content related to your business
- ◯ Created a piece of original content related to your business
- ◯ Spent time engaging with others social media posts
- ◯ Created a simple social media content calendar for the next week

Remember, the goal is not perfection but progress. The challenge is a way to practice using social media, to explore what works for you, and to start building habits that will help you grow your business.

CHAPTER 11
CUSTOMER SERVICE

Creating long lasting relationships

Customer Relationship Management (CRM) System

This helps streamline and manage customer data, track customer interactions, and automate some customer service tasks making the process more efficient for you and your customers.

Maintaining Consistent Customer Engagement

Customer engagement is vital for successful customer service. Whether it's via social media, email, calls, this offers a platform to answer customer queries and address their concerns promptly.

Encouraging and Implementing Customer Feedback

Actively seeking customer feedback, and implementing changes based on this, can provide invaluable insights into your business' strengths and areas that need enhancement.

Task Checklist

- [ ] Implemented a CRM System
- [ ] Regularly engaged with customers
- [ ] Collected customer feedback for ongoing improvement

CHAPTER 12 FINANCIAL MANAGEMENT

Sound financial management is crucial for the sustainability and growth of your business. Let's explore the basics.

Set up a separate bank account for your business

This helps you keep track of your business income and expenses, and makes tax time easier.

Monitor your business's financial performance

This includes your sales, expenses, profit margins, and cash flow.
Set up or purchase a simple Excel spreadsheet.

Stay on top of your taxes

Understand what taxes you need to pay, when they're due, and how to pay them.

Consider hiring a professional accountant

They can help you set up your accounting system, prepare financial statements, do your taxes, and provide financial advice.

Task Checklist

- ☐ Created a business bank account
- ☐ Monitored my business finances
- ☐ I understand my tax obligations
- ☐ I have researched accountancy services

CHAPTER 13
GROWTH PLAN

Scale your operations, team, and marketing efforts.

Identify areas for business expansion. This could involve offering new products or services, entering new markets, or tapping into new marketing channels.

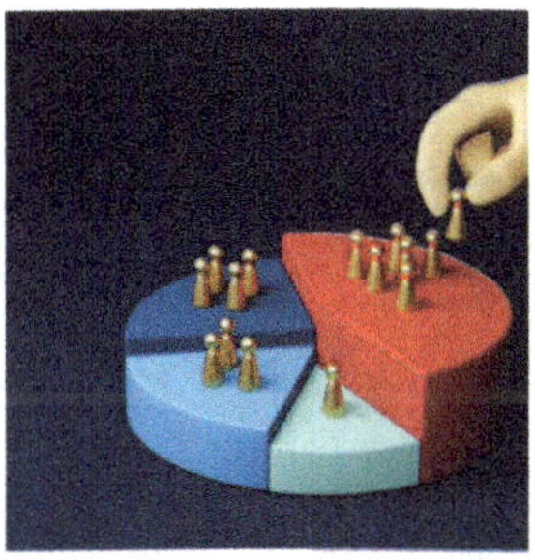

Stay updated with market trends. The business landscape can change rapidly, and staying on top of trends can help you spot opportunities for growth.

Regularly update your business plan. As your business evolves, your business plan should, too. Revisit the notes you made earlier in this course.

Hire more team members or outsource tasks as needed. As your business grows, you might need to delegate more tasks to focus on strategic planning.

CONCLUSION
FINAL CHECKLIST

Make sure you haven't missed anything!

- [ ] The Entrepreneur Mindset
- [ ] Identifying Your Niche
- [ ] Developing Your Business Idea
- [ ] Your Business Plan
- [ ] Building Your Website
- [ ] Understanding Search Engine Optimization (SEO)
- [ ] Registering Your Business
- [ ] Legal Considerations
- [ ] Set up Journal and Time Mgmt
- [ ] Marketing Your Business
- [ ] 5-Day Social Media Marketing Challenge
- [ ] Customer Service and Relationship Management
- [ ] Financial Management
- [ ] Growth Plan

Congratulations!

YOU MADE IT!

By reaching the end of this guide, you've taken a huge step towards starting your own online business. Remember that the road to entrepreneurship is a marathon, not a sprint. It's filled with challenges, but with determination, resilience, and the right resources, you're well-equipped to overcome them and succeed.

Entrepreneurship is a journey of constant learning and adaptation. Continue to seek new knowledge, learn from your experiences, and listen to your customers.

Your journey has only just begun. Best of luck on your entrepreneurial journey!

Did You Love This Book?

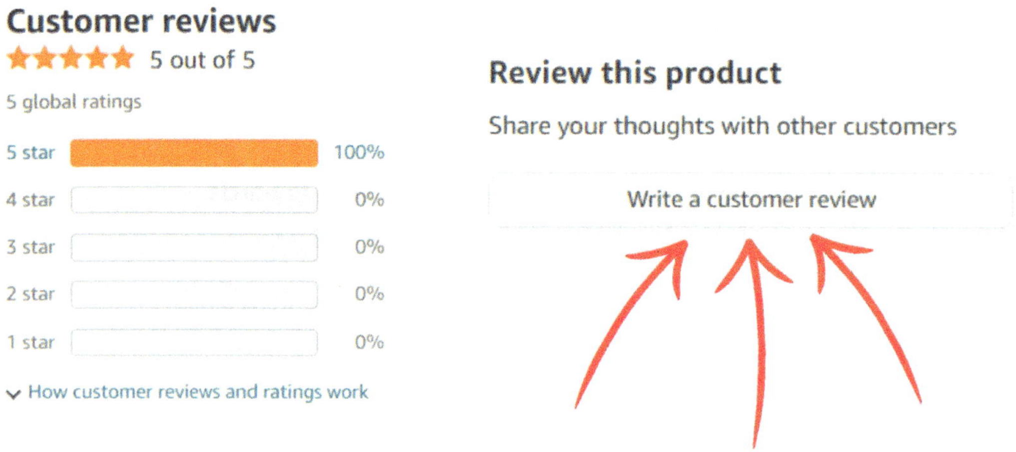

Your support would mean the world to me If you could take a moment to leave a short glowing review on Amazon to support this independent author, it would be greatly appreciated.

Kat Olsen's Other Work:

An Amazon #1 Top New Release in eCommerce

About Kat Olsen

Katheryn L. Olsen has over 25 years of life coaching experience, startup business consulting experience, and internet business building, marketing, and training experience. She has been a mentor to thousands over the years.

Katheryn was appointed the lead head coach for Robert G. Allen's Inner Wealth mentoring program, which spanned 18 months. She injected her S.O.S. principles to assist the clients in getting out of their own way and helping them avoid self-sabotage as they achieved more balance in the areas of "body, brain, being, time, people, and money."

In addition, she has developed, launched, and grown over 11 successful e-commerce businesses over the past five years. She has worked in dropshipping, print-on-demand, design, Etsy, and wholesale.

She has successfully consulted individuals and business owners internationally, such as Ritchie Hale of ELAH Group, in all phases of internet marketing strategies, all while identifying how and why her clients seem to get in their own way. She has discovered the Focused Expansion Rule.

In doing so, she has effectively brought together effective systems of self-analysis and practical, down-to-earth exercises to assist them in getting out of their own way. This leads to an effective and powerful harnessing of the Law of Vibrational Theory.

She has coached Olympic Gold Medalists, best-selling authors such as Cynthia Daddona, successful CEO's, construction workers, nurses, website designers, university marketing directors, internet business gurus, authors, info-preneurs, real estate investors and agents, restaurant owners, graphic artists, eBay merchants, event planners, network marketers, home-based businesses, stay-at-home moms and even other successful coaches.

Kat has been featured over the years in Chamber of Commerce publications, as well as online international publications such as Examiner.com, writing and publishing articles on how to launch and improve business on the internet as well as the self-help industry.

Made in the USA
Monee, IL
02 November 2026

67387945R00052